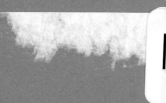

# KURDS
## IN BRITAIN

## Cath Senker
**Consultant: Sarbest Kirkuki**
**Photography by Chris Fairclough**

**FRANKLIN WATTS**
LONDON • SYDNEY

First published in 2005 by
Franklin Watts
96 Leonard Street
London
EC2A 4XD

Franklin Watts Australia
Level 17/207 Kent Street
Sydney
NSW 2000

A CIP catalogue record for this book
is available from the British Library.
Dewey number 305.891'597'041

Planning and production by
Discovery Books Limited
Editors: Kate Taylor and Laura Durman
Designer: Rob Norridge

The author, packager and publisher would like to thank the following
people for their participation in this book: the Sarbest family, the Kurdish
Cultural Centre, Broadwater Primary School, Mr Shepheard, Oli Centre,
Fresh Food City, Sait Akgul, Nazeeha Rasool.

Photo acknowledgements: All by Chris Fairclough besides: P6, Karim
Saheb/AFP/Getty Images; P7, Hugo Philpott/Getty Images; P10,
Howard Davies/Corbis; P14, Ed Kashi/Corbis; P20, Scott Peterson/Getty
Images;  P21, Reza;Webistan/Corbis; P26, Sion Touhig/Getty Images;
P27, Ferdhaus Shamim/Corbis

ISBN 0 7496 5884 3

Printed in Dubai

# Contents

# British and Kurdish

In Britain today, there are estimated to be between 70,000 and 75,000 Kurds, although there are no official figures. Most of them were not born here. They have come from the region known as Kurdistan, which stretches across Iran, Iraq, Turkey and small areas of Syria and Armenia.

## Kurdistan

Although Kurdistan is the homeland of the Kurdish people, it is not recognized as a state. The governments of the surrounding countries do not want to give up control of the region to create an independent Kurdish state. This has caused a lot of hostility in the region, and many Kurds have fled as refugees, not only to Britain but to other European and Middle Eastern countries.

The shaded part of the map shows Kurdistan, the area where most of the world's Kurds live.

When entering these countries, refugees are usually grouped under their country of origin. As Kurdistan is not a country, Kurds are often registered as being of Turkish, Iraqi, Iranian, Syrian or Armenian origin, and therefore, not distinguished from other people arriving from these countries. This is one of the main reasons that there are no official figures for the number of Kurds in Britain.

## Kurds in Britain

The largest Kurdish community in Britain is in London, estimated to consist of about 40,000 Kurds. Smaller groups live in other British cities, such as Cardiff, Manchester and Glasgow. About 14,000 Kurds are thought to live in Birmingham. Many are refugees, and so most communities have established community centres which give support and advice to those who have just arrived from Kurdistan, as well as those already living in Britain.

The Kurds have their own culture and language, and a large proportion of Kurds arriving in Britain cannot speak English. Community centres attempt to solve this problem by offering language courses, and some Kurdish settlers find work as translators, both for government and private institutions.

This Kurdish family, like many others, have settled in London.

**The Kurds have no friends but the mountains.**

*Kurdish proverb.*
*(Kurdistan is a mountainous region.)*

# Kurdish history

The Kurds have been fighting for an independent Kurdish state for nearly a century. Under the Treaty of Sèvres of 1920, the Kurds were supposed to be granted a homeland. The Turkish government refused to agree to the treaty, however, and in 1923 the plan was dropped. In the newly formed states of Turkey, Iran and Iraq, the Kurds were expected to abandon their traditional way of life.

## Kurds in Turkey

From the 1970s, the Kurds endured a wave of persecution in Turkey, Iran and Iraq. In Turkey, Kurdish national movement groups called for independence. In 1984, one group, the Kurdish Workers' Party (PKK), attacked the security forces. In retaliation, government forces arrested and tortured Kurds, and razed 4,000 Kurdish villages to the ground. The PKK ended its armed struggle in 1999 but the Turkish government continued to persecute Kurds.

A Kurdish family arrive in an refugee camp in Iraq, 1997. Since 1994, at least 14,000 refugees have fled to Iraq to escape fighting between the Turkish army and the Kurdish national movement groups.

## Kurds in Iran

In Iran, an Islamic Republic took power in 1979. It was strongly opposed to an independent Kurdistan. Armed conflicts between Kurdish nationalist groups and the government followed, in which about 55,000 Iranian Kurds died (1979–1992).

## Kurds in Iraq

Throughout history, Kurds in Iraq have fought for autonomy against the Iraqi governments, most recently that of Saddam Hussein (ruled 1968–2003). He used brutal methods to crush the independence movement, inflicting major defeats in 1975, 1988 and 1991.

**Members of Britain's Kurdish community celebrate as Kirkuk is liberated by the coalition forces from Saddam Hussein's regime in 2003.**

## ANFAL CAMPAIGN, 1988

**During Saddam Hussein's 1988 campaign against the Kurds, which included attacks with chemical weapons:**
- **182,000 Kurds were killed.**
- **More than 4,500 Iraqi Kurdish villages were destroyed.**
- **About 800,000 Kurds were deported from the Kurdish areas to camps elsewhere in Iraq.**

# Arrival in Britain

**Before 1974, small numbers of Kurds came to Britain from Iran or Iraq to study. Since the mid-1970s, there have been several waves of migration because of increasing conflict in Kurdistan.**

The majority of Kurds forced to flee have gone to other Middle Eastern states. Some have come to European countries, including Britain. Most of the earlier migrants had been active in the freedom struggle in Kurdistan, but in recent years many have come to escape the devastation and conflict in their home country.

Kurdish parents explain to their children why they had to flee their homeland and come to Britain.

## Iraqi Kurds

The biggest wave of Iraqi Kurdish refugees arrived in Britain following the Anfal campaign of 1988 (see page 7). After the 1991 Kurdish uprising against Saddam Hussein had been decisively crushed, the United Nations established a 'safe haven' for the Kurds in northern Iraq. However, life there remained insecure, even after the fall of Saddam Hussein in 2003, and Kurds continued to leave.

Food shops like this one cater for the many different ethnic minorities and nationalities living in Britain, including the Kurds.

## Turkish Kurds

From 1989, significant numbers of Kurds arrived in Britain from Turkey owing to the continuing conflict between Kurdish nationalists and the government (see page 6). In the past few years the situation in Turkey has improved but Kurds still struggle to gain access to equal rights.

## Iranian Kurds

Since the 1980s, Kurds have also come to Britain to escape Iran, where the prospects of achieving Kurdish independence are bleak. Kurds there do not have equal rights, they often live in very poor areas and their children are not educated in the Kurdish language. People who complain about their lack of rights face imprisonment.

# Refugees

The vast majority of Kurds living in Britain are refugees – some official and some unofficial. To be an official refugee you have to apply for, and be granted, asylum. At any time there are several thousand people waiting to find out if their claim to asylum will be accepted. Extremely few Kurds succeed in their claim.

## Unofficial refugees

Tens of thousands of Kurdish refugees who have been refused asylum still live in Britain. Life is extremely difficult for these unofficial refugees. They receive no benefits from the government, such as housing or cash support, and cannot work legally. Yet this situation is still preferable to returning to possible imprisonment, torture or death in Kurdistan.

Kurdish refugees from Turkey get together for a meal and a chat at the Kurdish Workers' Association in Haringey, North London.

## Dispersal policy

Until 1999, the majority of Kurds in Britain lived in London. In that year, the UK government introduced a new policy to disperse refugees around Britain. There are now Kurdish communities in Manchester, Glasgow, Birmingham, Cardiff, Swansea, Hull, Nottingham, Liverpool and other cities around Britain.

Not all Kurds are refugees. Some Kurds from Turkey are in Britain on work visas, and several thousand Kurds have become British citizens.

The Kurdish Cultural Centre in South London provides practical assistance and support for refugees and helps with legal matters.

## REFUGEES AND ASYLUM SEEKERS

When people who are in danger in other countries flee to the UK, they have to apply to the government for refugee status to be allowed to stay. This is called applying for asylum. The people who have applied and are awaiting the government's decision are called asylum seekers. If asylum seekers are refused refugee status they can be removed from the UK, but some hide from the authorities rather than face returning to their home country.

# Culture and entertainment

**Kurdish people are proud of their culture and determined to keep it alive. Throughout Britain, there are many Kurdish cultural centres for the support and education of the Kurdish community.**

## Language and culture

The Kurdish language has two main dialects. Kurmanji, written in Roman script, is used by the Kurds of Turkey, Syria and Armenia, while Sorani, using Arabic script, is the dialect of Kurds from Iraq and Iran. Despite living in different states and speaking different dialects, Kurds share a common culture based on their ancestral background and their desire for an independent Kurdistan.

This is a Kurdish poetry book written in Sorani.

Kurdish cultural traditions are passed on through the family. Many families try to speak only Kurdish in the home but this can be difficult as children growing up in Britain may prefer to speak English.

This Kurdish boy (left) speaks Kurdish at home with his family and English with his friends.

## Cultural centres

Kurdish cultural centres often run Saturday schools where children can learn Kurdish. They are a focus for Kurdish cultural activities, including art exhibitions, parties and Nowroz (New Year) celebrations. These events help Kurds to feel less isolated, and strengthen links in the community.

## Entertainment

Kurds enjoy the same entertainment as most other people in Britain. For example, watching satellite TV is popular. There are three main Kurdish satellite channels, ROJ-TV (formerly MED-TV), Kurdistan TV and Kurdsat, which enable Kurds in Britain to follow the news from Kurdistan. Other common pastimes are going to Kurdish restaurants and playing football.

**KURDISH CULTURAL CENTRE
AZADI LANGUAGE SCHOOL**

**Certificate of Achievement**

This is to certify that DLAWA SARBEST has passed all exams of class one
For the year 2003/2004, obtaining an average of 75%.
And accordingly he is going to start class two in year 2004/2005.

Anwar Ibrahim
Chairman
Of Management Committee

Sarbest Kirkuki
Project Coordinator

Kurdish Cultural Centre
14 Stannary Street, London SE11 4AA
Tel. 020 7735 0918    Fax. 020 7582 8894
E-mail: admin@kcclondon.org

# Religion
## and special occasions

**Religion is an intensely personal matter for Kurdish people, and does not form a major part of Kurdish identity. Most Kurds are Muslims. They don't have their own place of worship but will go to pray in their local mosque alongside other Muslims, and follow all the other Islamic customs, as well as some that are distinctly Kurdish.**

### Nowroz

The main Kurdish festival is Nowroz on 21 March, which means 'new day' in Kurdish. It is a celebration of the Kurdish New Year, the first day of spring, and the victory of oppressed people over tyranny. According to legend, over 2,500 years ago, a brave blacksmith named Kawa led a rebellion against the cruel ruler, King Zuhak. The people celebrated their freedom by lighting bonfires on hilltops.

**A Nowroz gathering in Britain. Nowroz is a joyful celebration for Kurds with music, dancing and traditional food.**

In Britain, Kurds and their friends gather and build bonfires. According to tradition, people dance around the fire. In North London, thousands of people join the festival – there is a huge bonfire and traditional music and dancing.

## Anfal Remembrance

All Kurdish communities have sad events to commemorate, too. For example, Iraqi Kurds gather each year on 16 March to remember the victims of the vicious Anfal campaign (see page 7).

## Kurdish clothing

Kurds often wear traditional clothing for festivals and cultural events. Kurdish men and boys wear a pair of trousers and a tunic top, called a shalwar. They sometimes wear a turban as well. The traditional women's outfit is called krasi kurdi, and consists of a dress, a waistcoat and a belt. Krasi kurdis come in lots of different colours, and are often decorated with sequins.

A Kurdish father and son wear traditional shalwars, while the mother and daughter wear their colourful krasi kurdis.

## KURDISH SOCIETY

**Various religious groups live alongside each other in Kurdish society. While most Kurds are Sunni Muslims, there are also Alevi Kurds, who follow a type of Shia Islam, and Yazidis and Kakayi, who have their own religion. Some Christians and Jews are found among the Kurds, too.**

# A Kurdish home

In Kurdistan, people usually live with their extended family. In Britain, however, Kurds often find they cannot afford homes large enough to house everyone, and so they cannot live in this way. In Kurdistan, traditional homes have a sitting room with no chairs, but here Kurds usually have Western furniture. Nevertheless, there are also Kurdish posters on the walls and Kurdish books on display.

## Food

The Kurds are proud of their cuisine and cook Kurdish food at home. Rice is the staple food, and various kinds of meat are enjoyed. Popular dishes include kebabs, made from grilled meat and onions, kofte (meatballs) and dolma (stuffed vine leaves). Many children also like the Western food they eat at school, so families may eat non-Kurdish food too.

A boy picks vine leaves from the garden so that his mother can make yaprakh, a traditional Kurdish dish.

Minced meat, rice, spring onions, dill and yogurt are wrapped in vine leaves to make yaprakh.

These children are eating a full breakfast with chickpeas, eggs, olives, yogurt and toast.

Kurdish people drink lots of tea. They have it in small glasses with plenty of sugar.

## Women

In traditional Kurdish society, women are responsible for the home and family while men work outside the home and are involved in public affairs. Many Kurdish women choose to stay at home when they come to Britain because it is what they are used to. However, some work outside the home or take advantage of the opportunity to study, which few women are able to do in Kurdistan.

"Living in London is very different from Kurdistan. I was a singer in Kurdistan and used to appear on TV a lot and spent my days socialising with friends and family. Here in London, there is not a big Kurdish community around me. We have to travel to meet up with friends and family now, which I find hard at times. I hope one day we can return to our home.

*Dlikosh Sarbest, London.*

# Childhood
## and growing up

Kurdish children in Britain grow up with Kurdish culture at home and Western culture outside. Kurdish parents generally take great responsibility for their children's well-being.

### Early years

Naturally, the birth of a baby is a cause for celebration; friends and relatives bring lots of gifts for the newborn. If possible, the baby sleeps in a traditional Kurdish cradle and is wrapped securely in blankets to ensure a good night's sleep, according to custom.

This little girl learns Kurdish as her first language from her parents.

" There is the British culture which I live in from morning until evening, and my Kurdish culture when I get home… I am divided between the two cultures and sometimes I think I don't belong to either of them. There are strong and weak points about both cultures. "

*Choman, a student in Britain from Iraqi Kurdistan.*

## Upbringing

Family values in Britain's Kurdish community are the same as in Kurdistan. Children are taught to respect their elders and it is completely forbidden to use swear words. Most families speak only Kurdish at home, so starting school

can often be hard for children. However, after two or three months children pick up English and school life becomes easier.

Kurdish parents allow children to spend time with friends as long as they know the friends and their parents. They are wary of dangers in the local area, such as crime and drugs, and, as other parents throughout Britain, do their best to bring up their children to act responsibly – and within the law.

This Kurdish boy (centre), working with his teacher, has mastered English and is doing very well at school.

A Kurdish boy plays a computer game with a friend who lives nearby.

# Weddings and funerals

Today, many young Kurds are allowed to choose who they marry, but in some traditional families, parents still arrange marriages for their children. It is not uncommon for Kurdish men to marry women of other nationalities, but it is not generally acceptable for Kurdish women to marry outside the community.

## Weddings

Wedding customs among British Kurds are similar to those in Kurdistan. The wedding is a lavish affair, usually held at a local community centre or town hall. The couple and up to 400 guests enjoy a wedding meal, followed by traditional music and dancing, and loud pop music. Patriotic Kurdish songs are often sung, alongside sad songs to remember the Kurds' suffering.

The bride and groom at a Kurdish wedding wait to greet all of their many guests.

# FINAL RESTING PLACE

**The majority of British Kurds take the body of their loved one back to Kurdistan for burial – often at huge expense. Whatever their station in life, Kurds have strong feelings towards their homeland. Even if they have not managed to return in their lifetime, they want a final resting place in Kurdistan.**

## Funerals

Funeral customs are based on those in Muslim countries. According to tradition, loved ones visit the cemetery every day for seven days after the burial. However, this can be difficult for working Kurds because of their commitments. Friends and relatives come to the family's home or local community centre to offer condolences and hear readings from the Qur'an.

A funeral procession in Derinje, Turkish Kurdistan. The body is placed in a simple white shroud, according to Muslim custom.

# Focus on London

London has by far the largest and most established Kurdish community in Britain and is home to up to 40,000 Kurds. (There are no official figures.) Kurds from Turkey are concentrated in Hackney and Haringey in North London. Kurds of Iraqi, Iranian and Syrian origin live all around London, mainly in areas with a high proportion of ethnic minorities.

## Community

London suffers from severe accommodation shortages, so housing is a big problem. Many newcomers live with friends and relatives for a long time until they find a place of their own. Kurdish people generally feel at home among the ethnic minorities in multicultural London, but may not have much contact with the majority of Britons.

South London is home to people of many different backgrounds, including Kurds.

These women are attending a Kurdish cookery class at the Kurdish Cultural Centre in South London.

Many older Kurds miss their close community in Kurdistan, where families, friends and neighbours look after each other. The Kurdish associations, of which there are about 25 in the city, play a vital role in providing support and a social network.

## KURDISH ASSOCIATIONS

The Kurdish Cultural Centre in South London provides Kurds with information on immigration and housing matters, organises cultural activities on a national level and helps Kurds in other cities to set up their own community centres. The Kurdish Community Centre in North London is also a focal point for cultural activity and provides information, advice, support and English classes for refugees in the area, who are mostly from Turkey.

Employees at the Kurdish Cultural Centre in South London.

# The world of work

Kurdish people are employed in a variety of economic activities. A few – especially well-educated men from Iraq – have highly paid jobs, for instance, in the IT sector or as doctors. However the majority are in low-paid work. Refugees awaiting the outcome of their asylum claim and those who are in Britain illegally are not permitted to work but often find employment in the 'black' economy.

Kurdish cultural centres rely on both paid and volunteer workers to run services for their community.

## Education and work

The kind of jobs Kurds do depends partly on their level of education on arrival. It also depends on how long people have been in the country. The longest settled speak better English, which makes it easier to find work. Even highly skilled refugees generally work in poorly paid jobs if they are recent arrivals. Large numbers of Kurds work long hours in restaurants, cafés and shops.

Local shops in Kurdish areas like this one are typical places of employment for Kurdish people.

## Hard work, low pay

Kurds from Turkey rarely speak English upon arrival in Britain and are generally poorly educated. They often take the lowest-paid jobs, such as in 'sweatshops' – unofficial clothing manufacturing units – where speaking English is not necessary.

## Self-employment

Some Kurds have set up their own businesses in Britain, for example running shops, restaurants and textile factories. One success story is B-Plan Information Systems, set up by two Kurdish brothers in Manchester, which has one several awards for small business enterprise. Businesses like this, along with Kurdish cultural centres, have contributed to the development of Kurdish communities within Britain.

> **For a lot of Kurdish people in London, their future [is] not guaranteed. They haven't got a job... It's not easy to live like this... people want to save some money, they want to have a shop, [be] self-employed.**
>
> *Kurd from Hackney, London.*

# Threats and tensions

Kurdish asylum seekers are at the sharp end of racism in Britain. The media and press have often provoked an unfair belief that asylum seekers are in Britain to claim free support and live in homes provided by the government. Verbal and physical attacks on asylum seekers have increased in recent years.

## Racism

Kurds also suffer from the rise in anti-Muslim sentiments since the attacks on the USA of 11 September 2001. Racist abuse and violence against Kurdish people are common in cities where they are recent newcomers, such as Swansea, Sunderland and Hull. At school, Kurdish children who do not speak English may be isolated and become the target of bullying.

Kurdish demonstrators, in Britain in 2001, protest against the government's failure to deal with the rise in racist attacks on asylum seekers in the country.

## RACIST MURDER

Kalan Kawa Karim was a 29-year-old Iraqi Kurdish refugee who had fled Iraq after being tortured under Saddam Hussein's regime. In 2004 he was living in Swansea. One night Karim was viciously attacked in the city centre by a racist and died later in hospital. The director of Swansea Race Equality Council commented that racist attacks had risen threefold since 11 September 2001, but that the problem was no worse than in other cities.

## Cultural misunderstanding

Some of the difficulties arise because many local people do not know about Kurdish culture and make no effort to communicate with their Kurdish neighbours and to get to know them. For example, Kurdish people take great offence if anyone swears at them, and this can cause tension and lead to violence. City councils, such as Hull's, have staged events to promote better community relations and cultural awareness.

The British government banned the PKK (see page 6) as a terrorist organisation in 2001. Many Kurds, like this demonstrator, saw the ban as an unjust attack on their people.

# Future hopes and fears

Kurdish people would like to be offered a warm welcome when they arrive in Britain, and to be treated with respect. They hope to play a useful role within British society while maintaining their own culture. Eventually, most hope to return to Kurdistan although many fear this will not be possible for some time.

## Return to Kurdistan

Kurds arriving in Britain feel a strong sense of belonging to Kurdistan. Political refugees, who may have escaped bombings and torture, feel a particular responsibility for furthering the struggle for a free Kurdistan. As time goes on they put down roots in Britain, but most Kurds hope to return to their homeland one day.

However, many second-generation Kurds who have been born in Britain may not be keen to return to a homeland that they do not know. This is why Kurdish parents try to maintain Kurdish culture and traditions whilst living in the UK, and to teach their children about Kurdistan. Most families in Britain still have relatives there and may take their children to visit for a family reunion.

**Many Kurdish parents living in Britain hope one day to return to Kurdistan with their families.**

## Positive steps

The British government and police force are working with Kurdish communities to raise awareness of the contribution that they make to British society. For example, in Manchester in 2004, the police met with representatives of the Kurdish community to improve relations between them and to give their support for the development of a Kurdish community centre in the city. They thanked the Kurds for the help that they have given police forces throughout Britain to combat crime and to improve public safety.

We are keen to emphasise that the Kurdish community works together with the police to tackle crime and improve community cohesion and safety.

*Police officer, Manchester.*

# Glossary

**Anfal** literally translates as 'the spoils'; the Iraqi government's 1988 campaign to try to bring the Kurds under control.

**asylum** protection that a government gives to people who have left their own country because they were in danger there.

**asylum seekers** people who claim the right to live in another country because they were in danger in their own land.

**autonomy** the freedom for a region of a country to govern itself independently.

**'black' economy** business activity that is done without the knowledge of the government so that people do not have to have contact with officials or pay tax.

**condolence** an expression of sympathy with another person's grief.

**deport** to force a person or people to leave a country or region.

**dialect** a form of a language which is specific to a region or social group.

**disperse** to spread over a wide area.

**ethnic minority** a group of people who have a different culture, religion, language or skin colour from most other people in their society.

**homeland** the region where a person was born. Some peoples, such as the Kurds and the Palestinians, do not control their own homeland.

**Islam** the religion followed by Muslims and based on the word of Allah (God) as revealed to the Prophet Muhammad.

**migration** the movement of people from one country or region to another.

**Muslim** somebody who follows the religion of Islam.

**nationalist** in the case of people without their own state, a person who wants their country to become independent.

**patriotic** inspired by pride in and devotion to one's country.

**persecution** the cruel or unfair treatment of a group of people, often because of their ethnic origin or religious beliefs.

**racism** prejudice towards people from certain races.

**refugee** somebody who takes refuge from war, persecution or disaster by going to a foreign country.

**Shia** one of the two main branches of Islam. Most people in Iran and Iraq are Shia Muslims while the majority of Kurds are Sunnis.

**Sunni** one of the main branches of Islam, which is followed by most Kurds.

**torture** to inflict severe pain on someone as a form of punishment or in order to make them say or do something.

**treaty** an agreement or contract between two or more states or rulers.

**United Nations** an organisation, founded in 1945, which aims to encourage international cooperation and peace. Today, it includes most of the countries in the world.

# Further information

This is a selection of websites that may be useful for finding out further information on Kurds in Britain.

**www.refugeecouncil.org.uk/**
British Refugee Council

**www.middleeastuk.com/com/kcc/index.htm**
Kurdish Cultural Centre

**www.guardian.co.uk/The_Kurds/0,2759,1929 81,00.html**
Articles about Kurds in Britain and Kurdistan.

**www.communitycare.co.uk/articles/article.asp ?liarticleid=42482**
About Kurdish people in Glasgow.

**Note to parents and teachers**
Every effort has been made by the Publishers to ensure that these websites are suitable for children, that they are of the highest educational value, and that they contain no inappropriate or offensive material. However, because of the nature of the Internet, it is impossible to guarantee that the contents of these sites will not be altered. We strongly advise that Internet access is supervised by a responsible adult.

# Index